THE G.I. SERIES

Screaming Eagles

The 101st Airborne
Division from D-Day to
Desert Storm

Lawrence Walter of the 502nd Parachute Infantry Regiment (PIR) poses for a photograph before a jump. Walter was one of the army's earliest paratroopers. This picture was taken prior to America's entry into the war. Walter is wearing the blue denim fatigue uniform, which began to be replaced by the green herringbone twill uniform in 1941. (JP)

THE G.I. SERIES

THE ILLUSTRATED HISTORY OF THE AMERICAN SOLDIER, HIS UNIFORM AND HIS EQUIPMENT

Screaming Eagles

The 101st Airborne Division from D-Day to Desert Storm

Christopher J. Anderson

Greenhill Books
LONDON

Stackpole Books
PENNSYLVANIA

Greenhill Books

This edition of *Screaming Eagles* first published 2000
by Greenhill Books,
Lionel Leventhal Limited, Park House, 1 Russell
Gardens, London NW11 9NN
and
Stackpole Books, 5067 Ritter Road, Mechanicsburg,
PA *17055,* USA

© Lionel Leventhal Limited, 2000

British Library Cataloguing in Publication Data
available

ISBN *1-85367-425-7*

Library of Congress Cataloging-in-Publication Data
available

DEDICATION

This book is dedicated to Carmen Gisi of B/4O1st and
all the members of E/506 who so patiently listened.

ACKNOWLEDGEMENTS

The author wishes to thank Raymond Denkhaus and
Ivan Ingraham for their help. Special thanks goes to
Jake Powers, without whose help this book would not
have been possible.

ABBREVIATIONS

JP – Jake Powers' Collection
NA – National Archives
USA – U.S. Army
CJA – Author's Collection
ML – Mike Lupo Collection
USAF – U.S. Air Force
CG – Carmen Gisi
PPA – Primedia Photo Archives

Design and layout by David Gibbons and Anthony A.
Evans, DAG Publications Ltd
Edited by Stuart Asquith
Printed in Hong Kong

SCREAMING EAGLES
THE 101ST AIRBORNE DIVISION FROM D-DAY TO DESERT STORM

On August 16 1942, General Order number one was issued by, then colonel, Don F. Pratt, announcing the activation of the 101st Airborne Division at Camp Claiborne, Louisiana. Three days later the division's first commander, Major General William Carey Lee, wrote to the men of his fledgling command and reminded them that as a new and untried formation, they had no history of their own to draw upon and would, through their deeds and actions, establish the traditions and reputation that would help mark a course for future members of the U.S. Army's airborne forces. *'The 101st Airborne Division has no history,'* Lee wrote, *'but it has a rendezvous with destiny.'*

The division had been formed just nine months after America's entry into World War II and was the second of the U.S. Army's new airborne divisions. It had been created in the wake of successful tests first performed by members of the Parachute Test Platoon, that had first been formed in June 1940, and later by the 501st Parachute Battalion, that was formed in September. The formation of these early parachute units had been inspired by the startling success achieved by German paratroopers in the earliest operations of the war. Although tested by the Russions, prior to the *Fallschirmjagers'* victories, the deployment of appreciable numbers of soldiers descending from the sky in parachutes had seemed like fantasy. While some visionaries, such as aviation pioneer Billy Mitchell, had realized their potential, most traditional-minded military officers considered paratroopers wholly impractical on the battlefield and gave the first small parachute formations scant consideration. It was perhaps fortuitous for the future of American airborne forces that the Axis powers were able to secure such stunning victories at the start of the war. Caught unprepared for the speed and lethality of German and Japanese offensive operations, American military planners faced with the task of building an army capable of defeating the Axis powers were more prepared to pursue ideas that just a few short years earlier would have been considered irrational. It is more fortunate still that the officer most responsible for overseeing the creation of that army, George C. Marshall, understood the potential of airborne forces. From the very beginning, William Lee,

Matthew Ridgway and other early airborne officers stressed that the new airborne soldiers were members of an elite organization. To foster this sense of *esprit de corps,* special items of clothing, equipment and insignia were developed that served to set the airborne volunteer apart from soldiers in more traditional 'leg' (non-jump qualified) outfits. First among these unique items was the famous Parachute Qualification Badge – 'jump wings.' Devised by William P. Yarborough (who later commanded the S09 PIB in the first U.S. combat jump of the war), one of the test platoon's first officers in early 1941, the wings were awarded after the successful completion of five jumps, one of which had to be made in darkness. In addition to his wings, the qualified parachutist was entitled to wear a light blue parachute disc on an overseas cap as well as the famous jump boots.

Although originally intended merely as a slightly higher version of the standard service boot, the jump boots soon came to identify the wearer as a member of an elite organization. Paratroopers zealously guarded their exclusive right to wear jump boots and woe betide any non-jump qualified soldier caught wearing them. In addition to the jump boots and other specialty insignia, paratroopers were also entitled to wear the cotton jump suit. The suit featured a jacket with four large bellows pockets and trousers with large thigh pockets. Again, although originally intended to be merely a functional item of clothing, the jump suit soon came to be a highly prized item among paratroopers. An indication of the suit's popularity among its wearers is found in the experiences of Dr. Terris Moore, an outdoor expert who was working with the Quartermaster Department to develop clothing and equipment for the airborne and mountain units. Moore traveled to Fort Benning, Georgia, to spend time with the paratroopers and discovered that the jump suit was seldom worn. It was believed by some that this indicated that the new suit was unpopular and should be withdrawn from use. On the contrary paratrooper officers told Moore. So highly valued were the jump uniforms that many paratroopers chose to jump in one-piece HBT coveralls rather than risk damage to their jump suits.

As the development of uniforms and equipment

continued, so did exercises to test training and doctrine. During several of the famous prewar U.S. Army maneuvers, the parachute and glider battalions (additional airborne battalions had been created after the 501st's success) demonstrated the impact that airborne soldiers could have on the battlefield. As airborne infantry units became more successful, army officials began to experiment with airborne artillery and engineer units. Meanwhile, they also continued the development of glider techniques. By the summer of 1942 all the elements were finally in place to form intact airborne divisions. In August 1942, the organization of the 82nd and 101st Airborne Divisions was authorized.

Each of the new airborne divisions was considerably smaller than a standard infantry division. While a regular division consisted of more than 15,000 troops, the new airborne divisions had just over 8,000 men. Airborne divisions were also more lightly equipped than other divisions, having fewer vehicles and lighter artillery. It was reasoned that the more lightly equipped divisions would be able to sustain themselves until reached by more heavily equipped forces.

Under the guidance of General Lee, the newly formed 101st Airborne Division spent the next year coming together as a division, improving physical conditioning – including the 2nd Battalion, 506th Infantry's epic march from Fort Benning to Atlanta, Georgia, a 118 mile march completed in just 75 hours – and preparing for future operations. Although they had yet to enter combat, the division's performance at training maneuvers in Tennessee and North Carolina had already begun to demonstrate that the early proponents of airborne warfare had not been mistaken. The preparation continued until August 1943 when the division was shipped to Camp Shanks, New York, for embarkation for Britain. After arriving in Britain in September, the division picked up the pace of training and on March 23 1944, took part in a massed jump before British Prime Minister Winston Churchill. Also in March, the division's commander, and the 'father' of the U.S. Airborne, General William Lee, was forced to resign after suffering a heart attack. Brigadier General Maxwell Taylor was appointed to command the division in what would be its first combat operation; the Allied invasion of Normandy, France.

On the evening of June 5 1944, paratroopers and glidermen boarded their aircraft and departed for France. The division's mission was to land on the right flank of the American invasion forces and to secure important bridges and terrain features around the town of Carentan that would isolate Germans defending Utah Beach and link up with ground forces advancing inland. The first American soldiers to land in occupied France were members of the division's pathfinder teams, commanded by Captain Frank Lillyman. Unfortunately the men of the division found themselves scattered all over the Cotentin Peninsula. It was in the chaos of the Allied airborne landings that the true value of the airborne soldiers became apparent. Isolated deep behind enemy lines, cut off from hope of immediate reinforcement, and often not knowing exactly where they were, the paratroopers of the 101st set out to find the war. Although often unrehearsed, the chaos that they and the members of the other Allied airborne divisions, sowed behind enemy lines was instrumental in securing Allied victory in Normandy.

During the first few days after the landings, division members fought a series of desperate actions aimed at halting German attempts to hurl Allied forces back into the sea. The division remained in combat almost continually until July 13, when it was finally withdrawn and transferred to England. By their performance in Normandy, the division had demonstrated that it had more than adequately met the demands of combat. Proving this came at a price, however and almost half of the division became casualties during the fighting in Normandy.

After a very brief opportunity to rest, the division began receiving replacements and preparing for their next operation. It was not only the new faces that began to change the division's appearance. That summer, the jump suit, first issued in 1941 and made famous in the battles of earlier that summer, began to be replaced by the new M1943 uniform. The new uniform was issued army wide and was intended to ease the problem of acquisition and resupply by doing away with various specialty uniforms. Ensuring standardization of appearance among all of the Army's soldiers was just the sort of decision that was bound to upset paratroopers. In an effort to preserve some of their individuality and to improve upon the new suit's carrying capacity, large pockets, resembling those found on the earlier jump suits, were added to the thighs of the new trousers. Perhaps the most damaging blow of all to the men of the parachute regiments was the decision to replace the distinctive jump boot with the highly unpopular M1943 Combat Service shoe otherwise known as 'two buckle boots'. Troopers bitterly resented having to give up their jump boots and many simply ignored the order to wear the new boots and preserved their jump boots for as long as possible.

Not all of the changes instituted after Normandy were bad. Having proved the absurdity of the notion that they were undeserving of the extra $50 dollars a month hazardous duty pay with their admirable combat performance and horrific casualties during the Normandy operation, Congress agreed to award glider infantrymen hazardous duty pay and most importantly, their own qualification badge which was similar to the jump wings.

The members of the division next had an opportunity to earn their pay when, as part of *Operation Market Garden,* they air-assaulted into Holland. The division was part of an intricate airborne operation that included landings by three Allied airborne divisions at three separate locations. The division's mission was to seize a series of bridges between the Dutch towns of Veghel and Eindhoven and to hold them until British armored units could pass over them on the way to relieving the British 1st Airborne holding the main road bridge over the Rhine River at Arnhem. On September 17 the division's infantry units braved heavy enemy anti-aircraft fire and landed in Holland. Unlike the earlier Normandy operation, the landing, which was carried out in daylight, went smoothly. Aside from heavy anti-aircraft fire, the division's units landed on, or close to, their designated drop zones. Almost immediately upon landing, members of the division were able to organize themselves and to move toward their objectives north of Eindhoven.

Although unable to capture all of the bridges intact, the division was able to secure the area assigned to them and hold it while British Royal Engineers reconstructed the destroyed bridge at Zon, midway between Eindhoven and Veghel. Despite the delay, the first British units were able to cross over an improvised bridge on the 19th.

For the next seven days, the division was forced to defend the narrow corridor it had seized against repeated German counter-attacks while British armored columns continued their desperate efforts to reach their trapped countrymen in Arnhem. The need to preserve the narrow corridor of land between Eindhoven and the Rhine in the wake of *Operation Market Garden's* failure required that after their positions between Eindhoven and Veghal had been reinforced, the division would be used elsewhere. The exhausted troopers spent a miserable month fighting to secure the 'island' between the Waal and lower Rhine rivers. The Screaming Eagles were finally relieved in November and sent to Mourmelon, France, to rest, refit and prepare for upcoming Christmas celebrations. Christmas plans were altered when news was received on December 16 1944, of a massive German offensive in Belgium that had ruptured Allied lines in the Ardennes. General Taylor was away in Washington DC at the time of the attack and acting divisional commander General Anthony McAuliffe received orders to leave Mourmelon and travel, as rapidly as possible, toward the breakthrough. By the morning of the 19th the bulk of the division had arrived at the critical crossroads town of Bastogne, Belgium, and had reinforced some other American units there. Soon, the Germans had the town surrounded and the epic siege was underway. So rapid had the division's departure from Mourmelon been, that many of the troopers were inadequately prepared for fighting in brutal winter conditions. Troopers inside the besieged city scrounged whatever GI clothing was available. Aware that the town was crucial for the continuation of their advance, the Germans threw massive counter-attacks against it for the next several days. Confident that they would be able to force the town's capitulation, on the 22nd the Germans asked McAuliffe to surrender the city. Unwilling to consider such a course of action, McAuliffe answered with the now famous response, '*Nuts!*' The Germans responded by stepping up their attacks, including, on Christmas Eve 1944, a massive aerial bombardment. On the evening of December 26th, after seven desperate days, leading elements of the 4th Armored Division broke through German lines and reached the city. After the siege had been lifted, the division took part in counter-attacks against the Germans. On January 18 1945, the division turned the city over to VIII Corps. On March 1 the division returned to Mourmelon and on the 15th, General Dwight D. Eisenhower presented the division, as well as Combat Command B of the 10th Armored Division and Reserve Command of the 9th Armored Division, with the Presidential Unit Citation for its heroic defense of Bastogne. It was the first time in the history of the United States Army that an entire division had been so honored. After the ceremony the division rejoined the advance into Germany, crossing the Rhine on April 25 and, on May 5 1945, reached Adolf Hitler's summer residence at Berchtesgaden where they were when VE-Day was announced. The atomic bomb detonations at Hiroshima and Nagasaki ended the war and the need to redeploy divisions from Europe. Instead of preparing for operations against Japan, on November 30 1945, the 101st Airborne Division was disbanded. In the division's last daily bulletin, Colonel Kinnard wrote. *'To those of you left to read this last daily bulletin, do not dwell on the disintegration of our great unit but rather be proud that you are of the "old guard" of the greatest division ever to fight for our country. Carry with you the memory of its greatness wherever you may go, being always assured of respect when you say, I served with the 101st'.*

The 101st ceased to exist, except for periodic activations as a replacement and training command until September 21 1956, when it was reconstituted as an airborne division and stationed at Fort Campbell, Kentucky. At the time of its reactivation, the division was used by the Army to test new airborne concepts, including becoming the first 'Pentomic' Division. It also served as the Strategic Army Corps' airborne division. Although not involved in combat operations, the division was called out by President Eisenhower to suppress civil disturbances in Little Rock, Arkansas, in September 1957 and later was prepared for a possible jump into Cuba in response to the missile crisis in 1962. Throughout this period the division was uniformed and equipped in a similar fashion to the rest of the army although the highly prized jump boots, now in black, had replaced the despised two buckle boots.

As America's involvement in the war in Vietnam increased, the 101st was called upon again. In July 1965 the division's First Brigade was deployed to South Vietnam's Central Highlands to relieve the 173rd Airborne Brigade. While deployed to Vietnam the brigade was involved in clearing Phu Yen Province. Successful in the Central Highlands, the First Brigade was later used throughout the country's four tactical zones, earning it the sobriquet, the 'Nomads of Vietnam.'

The entire division was reunited in November 1967, when the remainder of the division was deployed to Vietnam from Fort Campbell. In January 1968, in response to the unexpected Vietnamese TET offensive, units of the division fought in engagements throughout Vietnam; including one platoon from the Second Brigade, which was on the roof of the U.S. embassy in Saigon when it was attacked by Viet Cong guerrillas. Following TET, the Division launched *Operation Nevada Eagle,* its largest and longest operation of the war. *Nevada Eagle* lasted for more than 280 days and swept Thua Thien of most of the Communist troops in the province. Based on the overwhelming success of the 1st Air Cavalry Division, the army began to consider ways to expand on the helicopter's effectiveness. It was also becoming apparent that it was increasingly difficult to maintain jump-qualified divisions. Seven months after the 101st's arrival in Vietnam, the decision was made to take advantage of the increasingly significant role that helicopters were taking in combat operations by converting the 101st to an airmobile division. The division was now designated as the 101st Airborne Division (Airmobile) and its troopers were delivered to battle in UH1-Huey helicopters rather than parachutes.

In addition to changes in equipment and mission, during its time in Vietnam division members also began to receive new uniforms. Athough they originally deployed wearing the Army's olive green (OG) 107 utility uniform with black leather jump boots, it was quickly found that this uniform was ill-suited for use in Vietnam. As it became available, division members began to be issued with the tropical combat uniform and boots, the famous jungle uniform. This uniform consisted of an olive green cotton poplin jacket and trousers. The boots featured leather bottoms with nylon uppers. Ironically, the design of the new uniform had been inspired by the famous jump suits of World War II fame.

Despite its redesignation the division was able to improve upon its sterling reputation. In the spring of 1968 the division was involved in operations in Quang Tri and Thua Thien Provinces and subsequently at Hue. Later, the division took part in operations in the Dak To Highlands and further mission in Thua Thien Province. The division remained in Vietnam, taking part in *Operation Jefferson Glenn,* the last U.S. offensive operation in Vietnam, until 1972, when it was redeployed to Fort Campbell. More than 50,000 men, 4,011 of whom were killed in action, served with the division during its more than 1,500 days of action in Vietnam. One of the division's former opponents commented that of all the American organizations that he opposed during the war, the one that he feared the most was the 101st.

Two years after its return to the United States, in October 1974, the division was redesignated as the 101st Airborne Division (Air Assault). In recognition of this change in designation, Division Commander Major General Sidney B. Berry authorized an airmobile (later air assault) badge. The new badge featured a Huey helicopter superimposed over the wings found on the earlier glider and paratrooper wings. The air assault badge was officially adopted by the Army on January 20 1978 and, like the jump and glider wings, has since become a mark of distinction. Despite the loss of its jump status, the division continued to wear the airborne tab above the screaming eagle patch in honor of its origins.

The Screaming Eagles were not called upon again until the 1990s. After the fall of the Berlin Wall in 1989 many people believed that the demise of communism would mark an era of peaceful coexistence among nations. That belief suffered a blow in August 1990, when Iraqi dictator Saddam Hussein invaded and occupied the tiny nation of Kuwait. In response, a large international force was assembled in Saudi Arabia to halt any further Iraqi advance. The 101st Airborne Division (Air Assault) was among those units that deployed to the Persian Gulf. After repeated efforts to negotiate a settlement with the Iraqi leader had failed, on January 16 1991, Allied forces began *Operation Desert Storm* with an aerial bombing campaign. The air assault continued until February 24th when ground forces were launched against Iraqi positions in Kuwait. In the largest helicopter lift in history, 400 helicopters transported 2,000 members of the division into Iraq where they destroyed Iraqi columns trying to flee westward and prevented the escape of Saddam Hussein's trapped forces. Since the 1991 Persian Gulf War the division has continued to support U.S. Army operations around the globe.

From the earliest days of the parachute test platoons to the helicopter assaults of Vietnam to the massive airlift during *Operation Desert Storm,* the 101st has never ceased living up to the expectations of General William Lee who first recognized that the division had a *'rendezvous with destiny'.*

FOR FURTHER READING

Ambrose, Stephen E., *Band of Brothers.* Simon and Schuster, 1992.

Howard, Gary, *America's Finest.* Greenhill Books, 1994.

Rottman, Gordon, *US Army Airborne 1940–90.* Osprey 1990.

Katcher, Philip, *US 101st Airborne Division 1942-1945.* Osprey, 1978.

Rappaport, Leonard and Northwood, Arthur, *Rendezvous With Destiny.*

101st Airborne Division Association, *1965.*

101st Airborne Division, *The Epic of the 101st Airborne.* 101st Airborne Division, 1945).

Stanton, Shelby, *World War II Order of Battle.* Galahad Books, 1984.

Stanton, Shelby, *Vietnam Order of Battle.* Galahad Books, 1986.

Stanton, Shelby, *U.S. Army Uniforms of the Vietnam War.* Stackpole Books, 1989.

Right: Carl Fenstermaker, Rod Strohl, Forrest Guth, Amos Taylor from E Company, 506th Parachute Infantry Regiment (E/506), prepare for a training jump at Camp Mackall, North Carolina, in 1942. Rather than wear the M1942 Jump Suit, these men are wearing the first pattern (M1938) herringbone twill (HBT) coverall uniform. The use of the HBT coverall during training jumps was frequently practiced early in the war. (JP)

Below: Paul Rogers, Terrance Harris, Joseph Ramierez and an unkown trooper of E/506 return from a training exercise in North Carolina. The four men are wearing the HBT coveralls. The man standing second from the left has a 60mm mortar over his right shoulder and the man at right has a .30 Caliber Browning M1919A4 machine gun cradled in his arms. (JP)

Above: The crew of a C-47 works with a jeep operator to get his ¼ ton truck (jeep) on board the aircraft. Although experiments like this were conducted, jeeps were most frequently landed with the division's gliders. Unlike ordinary 'leg' infantry divisions, which had 612 jeeps, the more lightly equipped airborne divisions only had 283 of this highly versatile vehicle. (NA)

Left: A trooper prepares to jump from a C-47 transport aircraft. This photograph was obviously staged for the benefit of home front audiences. The standard procedure for exiting a C-47 in flight would have called for the trooper to stand in the doorway with both hands on the outside of the door. He is holding his static line in his left hand. After exiting from the plane, the static line would pull the cover off of his pack tray and deploy his parachute. (USA)

Above: A trooper of the 101st prepares to jump. Although a staged photograph, the paratrooper is equipped as he would be for the Normandy drop. The trooper has an Ml Rocket Launcher ('bazooka') slung over his left shoulder. Visible behind his reserve parachute is his Griswold Bag, which holds his M-1 Garand Rifle. Hanging underneath his reserve is a M1936 Canvas Field Bag, which would contain the trooper's personal items. (USA)

Above: Another photograph of the same trooper prior to the Normandy jump. Visible on his left shoulder is his 101st Airborne Division Insignia. Unlike many infantry units, troopers of the 101st frequently retained their divisional insignia during combat operations. Of special interest is the extra packet of cigarettes that he has taped to his left sleeve. Due to the unlikelihood of immediate resupply, troopers became very resourceful in carrying their basic needs into combat. (USA)

Above: Two members of the 2nd Squadron, 17th Cavalry, clear a landing zone (LZ) in Vietnam. The two troopers are wearing the ERDL ripstop camouflage uniform, issued in Vietnam 1967. Although originally intended to be worn by reconnaissance units, these popular uniforms more generally issued by 1969. (NA)

Left: Troopers from the 101st prepare to embark from the slaid of a UH-1 'Huey' helicopter during operations in Vietnam. Responding to the tremendous success of the helicopter in combat, in July 1969, the Army converted the 101st from an airborne to an airmobile division. (NA)

Above: Platoon leader Warren Look uses an AN/PRC25 radio to check for directions. The radio had a range of 3.5 miles. The Radio Telephone Operator (RTO) has attached the radio to the frame of his lightweight rucksack to ease carrying. The men of Look's reconnaissance platoon are all wearing the ERDL camouflage uniform. They are armed with M-16A1 Rifles. (NA)

Right: Members of Company L, 75th Ranger Regiment, salute during a ceremony in Vietnam. These men are all wearing the ERDL camouflage uniform. Of special interest are the 101st Airborne Division Patches, Ranger flashes, and helmet cover insignia. Unlike many other divisions in Vietnam that began to wear subdued divisional insignia on their tropical combat jackets, the members of the 101st retained full-color insignia These men have sewn 'Rangers' tabs over their divisional insignia. (NA)

Above: Recent replacements to the division in the late 1970s receive instructions from their platoon sergeant prior to a jump. The man at right has a subdued divisional insignia sewn to his left shoulder. The recruits are wearing the M1-Type II Parachutist helmet. The venerable Ml helmet, first introduced during the early days of World War II, remained the U.S. Army's standard helmet until the early 1980s. (USA)

Below: A 101st Airborne artillery crew prepares to fire their 105mm howitzer during operations in Saudi Arabia. The crew are all wearing the daytime desert camouflage uniform, known by the GIs as 'chocolate chips' with the Kevlar 'fritz' helmet, which began to replace the Ml helmet in the 1980s and is now standard. (USA)

A captain calls in for instructions during an exercise in Saudi Arabia. Both the captain and his RTO are wearing the 'chocolate chip' uniform. Both men, however, are wearing Personal Armored System for Ground Troops (PASGT) flak vests without the desert cover. The rapid deployment to Saudi Arabia meant that many troopers deployed to the desert with many woodland pattern camouflage items. (USA)

Above: Troopers of the 101st enjoy an oasis in the Saudi Desert during *Operation Desert Shield*. Most of these men are wearing chocolate chips. A subdued divisional patch is visible on the shoulder of the man at right. The brown rectangular packages on top of the makeshift table are 'Meals Ready to Eat' (MREs). The MRE is the third generation successor to the famous K ration of World War II. Like its predecessor, the MRE is a self-contained meal that can be eaten either hot or cold by soldiers in the field. (USA)

Right: A trooper conducts surveys in Saudi Arabia. Over his chocolate chip uniform he is wearing All-Purpose Lightweight Individual Carrying Equipment (ALICE). To guard against the Saudi Arabian dust, he has a pair of Goggles, Sun, Wind, and Dust. Due to the threat of an Iraqi chemical attack, the Allied forces in the Persian Gulf wore their gasmasks at all times. The carrier for this trooper's mask can be seen on his left hip. (USA)

Above: The communications section of the 502nd PIR model their new 'Suit, Parachutist' M1942 Jumpsuits. Several of these men are holding the airborne version of the early papier maché liner (identified by the thick rolled edge), which, unlike the standard infantry liner, was secured to their M1C Paratroopers helmet with a snap-fastener. (JP)

Right: Sergeant William Guarnere of E/506 at a stateside barracks building. Guarnere is wearing the khaki cotton service shirt and trousers with garrison cap. Guarnere's cap is piped with light-blue infantry branch of service braid. Although recommended for a DSC for his actions at Bre Court Manor, the recommendation was eventually downgraded to a Silver Star. Guarnere would later lose a leg during the fighting at the Bois Jacques. (JP)

Left: Sergeant Guarnere leads a physical training (PT) exercise at Fort Benning in 1943. Guarnere is wearing his jump suit with trousers 'bloused' over his jump boots. The troopers of the 101st placed a high value on physical fitness and while in training at Fort Benning, everything was done 'at the double.' Guarnere has sewn his sergeant's insignia on his right sleeve,. Originally embroidered, as the war progressed, insignia was sometimes stencilled onto the jackets. (JP)

Below: Headquarters section of the 501st PIR line up for a morning briefing during field training exercises. The men are wearing a variety of clothing including HBT coveralls, jump-trousers (man standing front row third from the right), briefs (second from right), and white boxers (right).

Above: A trooper with the 501st's mascot. This 'goat keeper' has a .30 Caliber M1A1 Carbine. Unlike the standard M1 Carbine, the A1 featured a folding stock. The folding stock carbine could be carried either in a holster or, as here, slung over the shoulder. The folding stock carbine was exclusive to the airborne forces and intended for use by officers and specialists. (JP)

Top right: Troopers of the 501st try to give their mascot a drink. Except for the man at left, all of these troopers are wearing HBT coveralls. The two men at right are wearing herringbone twill mechanics' caps. Note that no insignia is worn on the HBT utility uniform. (JP)

Right: Jerry Wentzel of E/506 stands fully kitted out prior to a training jump at Camp Mackall, North Carolina, in May 1943. Wentzel has taped his t-handle entrenching tool to his leg with friction tape. It was very important that anything that might catch or snag on a parachutes shroud lines was secured prior to a jump. Later in the war, many troopers shortened the handles of the shovel or used the M1943 folding shovel. Wentzel was killed in action on the evening of 5th June, 1944, when his plane crashed enroute to Normandy. (JP)

Top left: Trooper Paul Miller at home on leave in Chambersburg, Pennsylvania, in 1942. Miller is wearing the Olive Drab service jacket with wool mustard trousers and overseas cap. Although the service jacket was originally intended for use in the field, during World War II it was used primarily as a dress uniform. Miller has the General Reserve Headquarters insignia on his left shoulder. This insignia was worn prior to the formation of the division. (JP)

Above: Merle Lauer on home leave. He is wearing the service jacket and trousers with the leather garrison belt. The use of the leather garrison belt was discontinued in 1942. Lauer served as the assistant to the 506th's regimental dentist. (JP)

Left: The original caption on this photograph says that this trooper 'has just released himself on the shock harness.' Originally intended to simulate the shock of a parachute's opening, the use of the shock harness was discontinued when it was found that it was more dangerous – and caused more injuries – than actually jumping. (JP)

Right: Lawrence Walter of the 502nd prepares to be released from the 'shock harness' during the tower phase of training prior to the first parachute jump. Since Walter was not jump qualified when this photograph was taken, he is required to wear his trousers over his jump boots and not bloused, which was a privilege only accorded qualified jumpers. (JP)

Below left: Photograph of a 502nd trooper just seconds after jumping from the door of a C-47 on his first training jump at 1500 feet. The canopy of his T-5 Parachute is still in the parachute's tray. Seconds after this picture was snapped, the chutes static line would rip open the pack tray and deploy the parachute. The small dots on the ground are 2½ ton trucks. (JP)

Far right: A trooper models a fully packed T-5 parachute and harness prior to a jump. The white webbing on the rear of the parachute is the static line. Prior to jumping, the trooper would receive the order to 'stand up and hook up' and he would snap his static line onto an anchor cable that ran the length of the aircraft. (JP)

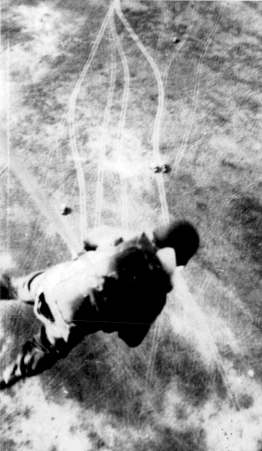

Opposite page, top left: A trooper of the 506th relaxes while off duty. This man is wearing the Parsons field-jacket (popularly known among collectors today as the M41 field jacket). While the jacket was worn in the field by 'leg' units, paratroopers used the jacket while in barracks. This man has sewn his regimental insignia to the left breast of his jacket. (JP)

Opposite page, top right: Two 506th troopers during a jump. A fellow trooper took this picture. The photograph illustrates the size of the parachute canopy when fully deployed. (JP)

Opposite page, bottom: Troopers of the 501st enjoy a 'songfest' during a training exercise. They all wear newly issued jumpsuits. When first issued, the cotton M1942 jump suit had a distinctive sheen to it. The photograph clearly illustrates the baggy thigh pockets on the trousers of the suit. (JP)

Above right: Officers and senior non-commissioned officers of the First Battalion, 506th PIR prepare for a jump at Toccoa. Many of the 506th's officers became jump qualified at Toccoa prior to the majority of the enlisted men qualifying at Fort Benning. Unlike all of the others who are wearing steel helmets, the man standing at right (1st Lt. Alex Bobuck) is wearing an olive drab wool A8 flight helmet. (JP)

Right: A 'camp barber' of the 501st during training maneuvers. Both men are wearing HBT coveralls over their jump boots. The man seated at right has a white towel draped over his shoulders. Later in the war, after olive drab towels began to be issued, white towels like this would have been uncommon. (JP)

Above: Colonel Howard 'Jumpy' Johnson (squatting at left), the commander of the 501st PIR, instructs one of his men in the proper method of digging a slit trench. Johnson was later killed in Holland. Colonel Johnson is wearing the M42 jump suit and he has attached an M1916 leather holster to a web pistol belt. (JP)

Left: Al Krochka, the photographer of the 501st PIR, during a training exercise. Krochka is wearing his M42 jump suit and jump boots. A folding stock carbine is slung over his right shoulder. An ammunition pouch for his carbine can be seen attached to the front of his pistol belt. The pouch could hold two magazines for the carbine. (JP)

Right: Senior non-commissioned officers and select men from the 502nd PIR prepare for General William C. Lee's final inspection. The men are all wearing the wool service uniform with jump boots. The Technician Fifth Grade at the left of the picture is holding his company's guidon. Each company had a guidon that featured a swallowtail pennant in branch of service colors with regimental numbers and company. (JP)

Below: A sergeant inspects members of Battery C, 377th Parachute Field Artillery Battalion (PFAB). Because of their role as artillerymen, all of these men are carrying the folding stock carbine, the holster for which is visible on the right hip of the inspecting sergeant. Several of the men also have letdown ropes attached to their equipment. These ropes were intended to be used by troopers who became stuck in trees during landing. (USA)

Below: Headquarters Company, 506th PIR, pass in review. The men all wear their '42 jump suits with jump boots and helmet liners. Just visible on the left sleeve of several men in the front rank is the white medics' brassard. These brassards were not often seen during combat operations. (JP)

Above left: Members of the 377th PFAB get into their T-5 parachute harnesses. They are standing in front of the legendary C-47 Sky Train. The C-47 was the workhorse of the Allied Air Transport Command. During operations, a Sky Train could carry twenty fully equipped paratroopers and their equipment into combat. (USA)

Left: Airborne artillerymen prepare their weapons for a jump. The parachute artillery battalions were equipped with the 75mm Pack Howitzer. Thirty six of these guns were assigned to each airborne division. The 75mm could be disassembled, placed in specially designed aerial delivery containers (pictured here) and dropped from bomb racks attached underneath the wings of the C-47. (USA)

Right: John Obergoss, a medic with the 506th PIR, is wearing a modified T-5 parachute harness. The T-55 usually buckled with chest clips, but after experiments with the British X-Type Parachute, many T-Ss were modified with push and turn buckles. This later model of the T-5 also features the olive drab webbing, which replaced the white webbing found on earlier harnesses. (JP)

Left: A 101st corporal stands smartly at attention and answers questions for British Prime Minister Winston Churchill during an inspection prior to the Normandy operation. The corporal is wearing all of the equipment with which he will later jump. Visible on his right thigh is a demolitions bag containing eight sticks of TNT. (CJA)

Below: Paratroopers enter Saint Marcouf on the morning of June 7, 1944. These heavily laden troopers are all armed with semi-automatic M-1 Garand rifle, the standard weapon of all American forces. Two of the three have attached their bayonets. On their backs these three troopers all have attached the M1936 musette bag to carry a few personal effects. (USA)

Above: Troopers proudly display one of their first trophies taken in Normandy. The picture illustrates the variety of equipment worn by members of the 101st during the fighting in Normandy. The paratrooper standing third from the left has festooned himself with hand grenades. To carry ammunition from his rifle, he has attached 'rigger pouches.' These small pouches were obtained from the air corps, or, more commonly, manufactured by unit parachute riggers. (NA).

Right: Corporal Darrell 'Shifty' Powers was described as one of the best marksmen in the 506th PIR. Powers is wearing olive drab service jacket and trousers. On the left sleeve of his jacket Powers has his rank insignia over which is the 101st's famous 'Screaming Eagle' patch. Underneath his jacket Powers is wearing a khaki cotton service shirt and tie. (JP)

Upper left: George Holmes of the 502nd PIR smiles for the camera. Holmes is wearing the olive drab wool garrison cap with light blue infantry piping. Holmes has affixed a first pattern parachute insignia on the right side of his cap,. These insignia, worn on the right side of the hat by enlisted men and the left by officers, featured a white parachute on a background in the branch of service color (in this case light blue). (JP)

Left: Ernest Labadie was a medic in the 502nd PIR. Labadie is wearing the wool service shirt and jacket with a mohair khaki tie. The photograph shows the proper method of wearing insignia and decorations on the service jacket. Note that Labadie wears his jump wings (visible on his left breast) over his campaign ribbons. (JP)

Above: Brigadier General Anthony McAuliffe, 101st Divisional Artillery Commander, gives last minute instructions to troop carrier pilots prior to the Holland operation. McAuliffe is wearing a yellow B4 'Mae West' life preserver over his M1943 field uniform. Note the oilskin American flag sewn to the right shoulder of McAuliffe's jacket. (USA)

Left: Headquarters Company of the 501st PIR at the conclusion of the Normandy campaign. Of special interest is the M1943 combat service shoe, known as 'two buckle boots' being worn with the earlier M1942 jump uniform. Paratroopers bitterly resented having to surrender their cherished jump boots in favor of the new 'two buckle boots' and most troopers continued to wear their jump boots for as long as possible. (JP)

Left: The sky fills with parachutes during *Operation Market Garden*. As troopers exit low flying transport planes, curious Dutch farm animals examine Waco CG 4-A gliders that have landed earlier. The CG-4A was the most frequently used glider in American airborne operations. Towed behind a C-47 until its final approach, the CG-4A could deliver 15 fully equipped glider troops, or 5,200 pounds of equipment, to the battlefield. (NA)

Opposite page, bottom: Glider men, most likely members of the 327th Glider Infantry Regiment (GIR), drive their jeep from the interior of their badly damaged Waco. Unable to drop by parachute, the division's jeeps were brought in by glider. After landing, the nose of the Waco could be raised to ease unloading. The photograph illustrates the fragile nature of the glider. (NA)

Below: Prior to take off, members of the 101st Divisional Headquarters Company (distinguished by the white square visible on the helmet of the kneeling trooper) pose in front of their Waco. These men are all wearing newly issued M1943 Combat Uniform. The Holland operation was the first time that the 101st used the new uniform, which replaced the popular M1942 jump uniform. (USAF)

Left: Don Moone (right) and Earl 'One Lung' McClung enjoy the hospitality of civilians in Eindhoven, Holland. Both men are wearing M1943 combat uniforms. Moone has laid a clip of ammunition for his M-1 Garand rifle and several MK2A1 fragmentation grenades on the lip of his foxhole for quick access. (JP)

Right: Members of the 326th Airborne Medical Company examine their damaged 1 ton 6x6 ambulances at Nijmagen during *Operation Market Garden.* Despite their airborne status, all of these men seem to be wearing the early Parsons (M41) field jacket. (USA)

Below: Immediately after landing in Holland troopers of the 501st PIR head toward their rally point. In airborne operations, it was critical for airborne units to rally their scattered men as quickly as possible. These men are all wearing the M1943 field uniform. Two of the marching men have their parachute first aid pouch tied to their helmet nets. These disposable first aid packets were worn in addition to the first aid packet worn on the ammunition belt. (USA)

Below: Members of the 101st return to their positions during the Battle of the Bulge. Other than the pockets added to the trousers of the man at the left and right, there is little to identify these men as members of an airborne unit. The man at left has clipped his collapsible canteen cup to his pistol belt. All three men are carrying improvised bedrolls over their shoulders. The winter of 1944-45 was the coldest on record. (USA)

Left: Three members of B Company (from left to right, Al Vaughn, Carmen Gisi, and Ed Benetueski), 401st Glider Infantry Regiment, pose for the camera. Vaughn still wears a pair of the earlier jump boots; while Gisi has been lucky enough to obtain a pair of the very rare canvas and rubber arctic overshoes. Both Vaughn and Gisi M3 have fighting knives strapped to their legs. Vaughn also sports a captured German P-38 pistol. (CG)

Below: The smiles on the faces of Sergeant Richard Gill (left) and Mike Compana (right) conceal the precarious nature of the situation. Both men are wearing M1943 field jackets and trousers. The trousers have been modified with the addition of thigh pockets. Gill has an airborne first-aid packet attached to the front of his helmet. This photograph was taken at the height of the Battle of the Bulge. (CG)

Opposite page, top: Members of the 101st move out from Bastogne to positions outside the city. Many of these men are wearing the M1939 enlisted wool overcoat. Although members of the 101st did not often wear the overcoat in combat, the extreme cold and lack of adequate clothing meant that many troopers were forced to wear the bulky overcoat during the Battle of the Bulge. (USA)

Opposite page, bottom: Members of the division sing Christmas carols during the siege of Bastogne. While two of these men wear the M1943 field jacket, the two troopers with their backs to the wall wear the earlier Parsons field jacket. The man at left is wearing his under a wool overcoat. (USA)

Left: Bedraggled members of B Company, 401st Glider Infantry Regiment, during the Battle of the Bulge. All are wearing M1943 combat jackets and trousers. Frank Almovich (kneeling at right) has a fighting knife strapped to his lower leg and tucked into the top of his arctic overshoe. Almovich was killed in action shortly after this picture was taken. (CG)

Right: Private First Class W.J. Ottersbach from the 327th GIR cleans his rifle during the Battle of the Bulge. Ottersbach is wearing several layers of clothing underneath his field jacket for extra warmth. Visible underneath his helmet is the visor of the wool M-1941 wool cap, known universally as a 'jeep cap.' He is also wearing the leather palmed wool glove, which was first issued with the new M1943 field uniform. (USA)

Below: Members of the 401st examine a captured German staff car. All are wearing M1943 field jackets and trousers although only two seem to have the divisional insignia sewn to the sleeves of their jackets. The man kneeling with his back to the camera is a non-commissioned officer, which is determined by the white horizontal line visible on the back of his helmet. (CG)

Opposite page, bottom: Wounded of the 101st receive medical attention at an improvised field hospital in Bastogne. The trooper with his back to the camera is wearing a pair of bibbed winter combat trousers (known as tanker coveralls) over his other clothes. Since hospitals within the besieged city often came under enemy fire, he has also wisely decided to continue to wear his helmet. (USA)

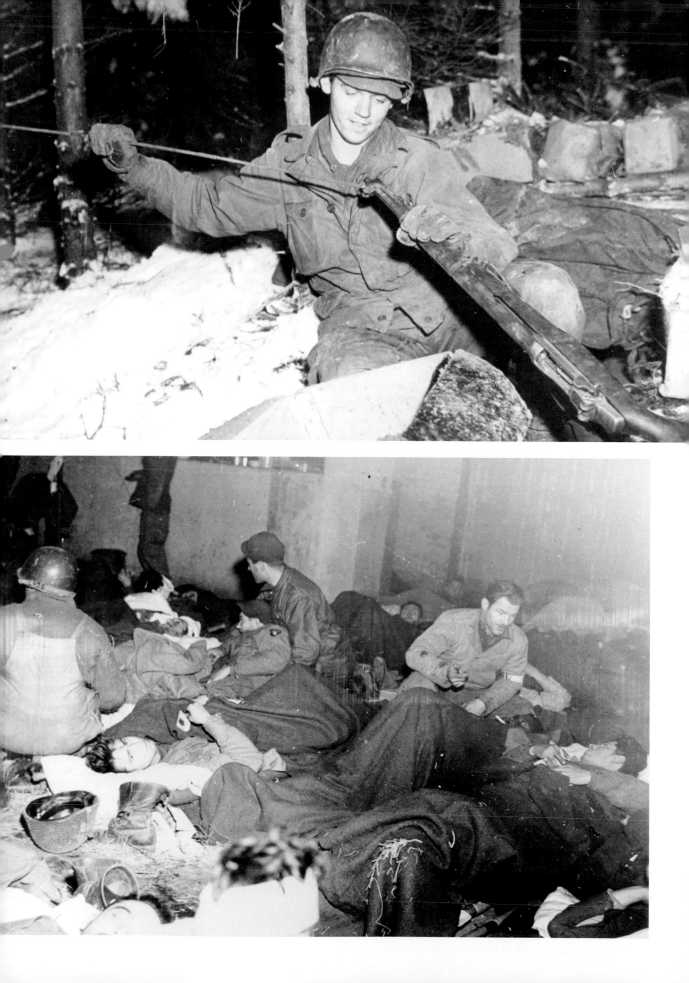

Above: Arno Whitebread (left) and Martin Chisholm (right) sight in a .50 caliber machine gun. Both men are members of the 327th GIR. The 327th's unit insignia (a white club) is just visible on the side of Whitebread's helmet. Although the .50 caliber machine gun was capable of a devastating 450-575 rounds per-minute rate of fire, its 82lb weight meant that it was infrequently seen in the more lightly equipped airborne division. (USA)

Left: Two members of the 777th Anti-Aircraft Artillery Battalion (left) warm themselves next to three members of the 101st. The photograph illustrates that at Bastogne, there was little to distinguish members of the 101st from the town's non-airborne defenders. Two of the 101st troopers have been lucky enough to obtain arctic overshoes, which they are struggling into. (USA)

Above: On Christmas Day 1944, three members of the division – two of whom appear to be NCOs – survey the wreckage of Bastogne. Although they were able to prevent the Germans entering, the town was destroyed. (USA)

Above left: Troopers move up through Houffalize during the first days of the Battle of the Bulge. Most of these men are wearing the wool overcoats and jump boots. Of special interest are the improvised bedrolls being carried by two of the men. The heavy equipment in the field opposite the road belonged to one of the regular infantry divisions in the area. Airborne divisions did not have self-propelled artillery as part of its table of organization. (USA)

Left: Troopers of the 101st move toward the frontline after being rushed to Bastogne. These men all seem to have been transported to the front in British trucks. Most of the troopers are carrying improvised bedrolls and many are wearing wool overcoats. (USA)

Right: Troopers of a heavy weapons platoon advance toward their positions in Bastogne. Three of the men in the column are carrying M9A1 Rocket Launchers (bazookas) while the man at the front is carrying rockets for the bazooka in their cardboard tubes at his chest. Although inadequate in stopping German tanks, the bazooka was effective against enemy soft skinned vehicles. (USA)

Below: Major General Taylor (left) discusses the defense of Bastogne with his divisional artillery commander Brigadier General Anthony McAuliffe (right). Taylor was in Washington, D.C. when the battle began and McAuliffe commanded the division during the worst days of the siege. It was McAuliffe who uttered the famous pronouncement '*Nuts*' in response to German demands to surrender. The insignia of the divisional artillery is stenciled to the side of McAuliffe's helmet. McAuliffe is wearing an Army Air Corps B-10 Flight Jacket. (USA)

Below: Division commander Major General Maxwell Taylor (second from the right) greets his officers in front of a 'Battered Bastards of Bastogne' sign after the 4th Armored Division had broken through encircling German troops and ended the siege. Taylor has headquarters insignia stencilled to the side of his helmet and two stars affixed to the front. He is wearing an Army Air Corps B-11 Winter Flying Jacket. (USA)

Left: Troopers of the 506th pass a road sign directing them toward Berchtesgaden in April 1945. After the Bulge, the division served with the 7th Army and finished the war at Adolf Hitler's mountain retreat at Berchtesgaden. (USA)

Below: Members of the 506th PIR search German houses in Landsberg, Germany. After arriving at Berchtesgaden, members of the division searched the surrounding areas for die-hard Nazis in hiding. The troopers are all wearing M1943 uniforms. A German dagger and a pair of binoculars are visible on the left side of the soldier at right. The insignia for the 506th (a spade) is stencilled on his helmet. (USA)

Above: General Maxwell Taylor (on reviewing stand in garrison cap) presents unit citations to a platoon from the 02nd PIR, 506th PIR, and 327th GIR on the grounds of Hitler's Berchtesgaden estate. The division's flag can be seen next to the United States flag. All of the troopers have been issued with new short wool field 'Ike' jackets for the ceremony. (USA)

Below: In March 1945 General Maxwell Taylor (second from the left) presents citations to the different companies and regiments of the division for their participation in the Normandy operation. The larger flags are regimental standards (including the non regulation white, 501st PIR flag), the smaller pennants are company guidons. The photograph provides a good example of the various unit identification symbols painted on the sides of helmets. (USA)

Left: Major Richard Winters, in a photograph taken at Zel-am-See in Austria, June 1945. Winters had begun his service as a lieutenant in E/506. Buy the end of the war he had risen to command of the company and, at the end of the war, was promoted to major. H is wearing an Ike Jacket with division insignia on the left shoulder. Visible on his left epaulet is his rank insignia and, above that, the 506th distinctive insignia. (Richard Winters)

Below: The last jump of the 506th Parachute Infantry Regiment at Zel-am-See whilst waiting shipment home. Not long after this photo was taken the unit was disbanded and the remaining personnel were either sent home of transferred to the 82d Airborne Division. (JP)

Above: Members of the 101st pose for a picture with some Army nurses in front of the Arc de Triomphe in 1945. All but one of the troopers is in Class A uniform, which consisted of the four pocket service jacket, bloused trousers and jump boots. Of special interest is the jacket of the Technician 5th Grade at the center of the picture. He has outlined his divisional patch in shroud line material taken from a discarded parachute. Such embellishments were common in the 101st. (JP)

Below: Pathfinders from the 506th PIR at the end of the war. Top row, left to right: Lt Shrable Williams, John White, John Agnew, Lochman Tillman, Charles Perllow, James Benson. Bottom row, left to right: unknown, unknown, Paul Miller, William Goad. The pathfinders were an elite group of men designated to jump ahead of the rest of their regiments to locate landing zones. The winged pathfinder insignia is visible on the left sleeve of these men. (JP)

Top Left: Frank Lillyman, the father of the 101st's pathfinders, in an official photograph taken just after World War II. Lillyman is wearing a tan worsted wool officers' uniform with khaki cotton shirt and black tie. Of special interest are Lillyman's Master Parachutist wings. The arrowhead affixed to the wings is in recognition of Lillyman's participation in the Normandy operation. (JP)

Top right: Floyd Talbert is wearing a Parson's field jacket with the 506th PIR patch on the left breast. The clearly distinguished stitch lines indicate that this jacket has only just been issued. Exposure to the sun would have quickly faded this stitching to more closely match the jacket's cotton poplin material. (Talbert family)

Left: Massachusetts native David Lovell served as the 501st's regimental 'Pigeoneer'. He jumped into Normandy with carrier pigeons in addition to the rest of his equipment. On his return home he posed for his mother in his Ike Jacket, wool trousers and jump boots. Overseas stripes – Hershey Bars – are visible on his left sleeve. Each gold stripe signified 6 months overseas. (JP)

Above: Paul Miller (left) with an unidentified friend in the south of France in 1945. Visible on the left sleeve of the friend's Ike jacket is a pathfinder patch and a divisional insignia with a shroud line border. Interestingly, Miller's friend is wearing his jacket without a tie, a practice that would have been frowned upon by all but the most forgiving officers. (JP)

Above: Two troopers of the 506th PIR work on a foxhole. The two men are wearing the green cotton utility uniform. The cotton utilities were developed at the end of the Korean War to replace the HBT uniform. The color of the uniform was olive green (OG) 107. In a departure from World War II practice, divisional insignia was frequently worn with the utility uniform. (NA)

Right: Lieutenant Colonel Frank Stanley of the 326th Airborne Engineer Regiment prepares for a jump during a 1958 training mission. The Colonel is wearing the green utility uniform with the M1951 field jacket. Stanley is utilizing a T-7 parachute, which replaced the T-5 used during World War II, for his jump. Note the divisional insignia painted onto the tail of the plane. (NA)

Above: A trooper of the 2nd Battalion, 502nd Infantry Regiment (Airmobile) trudges up a hill in Vietnam. This man is wearing the M1956 individual load bearing equipment with a very full 'butt pack' visible on the rear of the harness. Not long after arriving in Vietnam, members of the 101st discovered that the butt pack was unsuitable for operations and replaced it with the lightweight rucksack. (NA)

Below: Troopers of the 502nd keep a sharp eye out for the enemy around Deo Mang Pass in August 1965. This trooper has camouflage helmet cover secured with the cover's elastic band over his M1 helmet. These bands were frequently used to secure small items, such as cigarettes, that the soldier wanted to keep dry or readily accessible. (NA)

Above: A trooper of the 502nd scans the horizon for the enemy. He has the plastic glasses case for a pair of sunglasses attached to the elastic band around his helmet. None of these men appear to have had an opportunity to have their divisional insignia sewn to the left sleeves of their jackets. (NA)

Below: UH-1 Hueys bring men and supplies into a landing zone. The Huey helicopter was the workhorse of the Vietnam War and replaced the C-119 as the 101st Airborne's primary means of aerial insertion. Supplies are being loaded onto an M274 mechanical mule for transportation to the men who have already left the Landing Zone (LZ). (NA)

Upper left: A mortar crew quickly unloads from a hovering Huey helicopter. These men have already lifted the base plate for the massive 4.2 inch mortar. Although capable of delivering heavy rounds at targets more than 5,000 meters away, its weight, 672 pounds, meant that it was not very practical for many operations in Vietnam. (NA)

Lower left: Colonel Smith of the Second Battalion, 502nd Infantry, establishes a command post at Deo Many Pass in November 1966. Radio telephone operators equipped with AN/PRC-25 radios surround Smith. The cluster of fully extended radio antennas would indicate that the colonel is not alarmed about attracting enemy fire. (NA)

Above right: Members of the 502nd board LST 587. The troopers bear much of their equipment attached to their M1956 load bearing equipment. Each of the front pouches visible on the man facing the camera contains magazines for his M16 rifle. He has clipped two M26A1 fragmentation grenades to the sides of each pouch. (NA)

Right: An instructor examines the weapons of division replacements who have just returned from a training exercise. Although these replacements are all equipped with M14 rifles, they will receive M16s when they finally reach their units. The instructor is wearing the trousers to the tropical combat uniform with the replacement center's distinctive black t-shirt and baseball cap. (NA)

Above: Two troopers in tropical combat uniform load a wounded Vietcong guerilla into a Huey. One of the Huey's crewman, watching over the two men from the interior of the helicopter, has painted the front of his AFH-1 Aviation helmet with a personalized message. (USA)

Left: An exhausted trooper trudges up a hill. This man has used the laces of his jungle boots to eliminate the baginess of his trouser legs that would otherwise easily become entangled in dense underbrush. He has stuck a spare M16 magazine inside the elastic band around his helmet. (USA)

Four of the 101st's M114A1 155mm howitzers are readied for action. The 155 was the heaviest towed artillery piece that the Americans used in Vietnam. Each of the division's two 155 battalions was equipped with 18 of these heavy guns. Also visible in this picture are some of the elaborate fortifications that would be constructed at more fixed positions. Much of the construction at this position seems to have been carried out using empty wooden ammunition boxes. (USA)

Top: Members of the 327th Infantry (Airmobile) open up on enemy positions during *Operation Carentan II* in 1968. The man at the center is firing the M60 machine gun. The M60 was a general purpose machine gun with a 600 round a minute rate of fire. It was used as the squad automatic weapon throughout the Vietnam War and replaced the earlier Browning M1919A6 .30 caliber machine gun. (NA)

Above: An M60 machine gunner keeps a sharp eye out from his position in the A Shau Valley in September 1969. This trooper has laid a 100 round belt of the disintegrating link 7.62 mm ammunition along the log that he is resting his gun on and another on the ground at his left. Although its rate of fire was impressive, the weapon's weight meant that this trooper was, no doubt, relieved to have his gun in a fixed position. (NA)

Left: Three helicopter crewmen (left to right, SP4 Kline, WO Abner, WO Sibley) from B Company, 101st Aviation Battalion, await orders at Firebase Birmingham. Kline is wearing an M1965 field jacket over his Nomex fire retardant flight coveralls. He is also wearing black leather jump boots. Aviation personnel frequently wore all leather boots, which were more fire retardant than the nylon jungle boots. (PPA)

Left: Brigadier General Willard Pearson addresses members of the division prior to the start of *Operation Eagle Bait* in June 1966. Pearson is wearing a second pattern jungle jacket, which featured shoulder epaulettes and concealed buttons. A subdued nametape is visible above his right breast pocket. The audience seems to be from two separate units. The men on the left are all wearing special 'Tiger Stripe' fatigues, which were worn by the division's Long Range Reconnaissance Patrol (LRRP) units. The unit to their right are all wearing ordinary fatigue uniforms. (NA)

Left: A trooper of the 101st reads a captured propaganda leaflet. He is wearing the M69 flak vest. This vest, which was made of multiple layers of ballistic nylon, replaced the earlier M1952 flak vest. Although they provided the wearer with additional ballistic protection, their extra weight meant that they were very hot and uncomfortable to wear. Most men simply did without. (NA)

Right: Members of D company, 501st Infantry are treated for wounds received near Tam Ky in August 1969. The men are all wearing the third pattern jungle fatigues, which featured concealed buttons and no epaulettes. The man standing at left has slung a disposable bandolier of M16 ammunition over his right shoulder. Each of these bandoleers could hold seven, 20 round, magazines. (NA)

Right: Members of the 326th Engineer Battalion work to clear mines from a road in Vietnam. Although most of the men are just wearing the normal fatigue uniform, the man operating the mine detector has wisely chosen to wear the M1952 flak vest. The full color divisional patch is clearly visible on the shoulder of the man standing second from the right. (NA)

Above: Sergeant Robert L. Robinson draws a parachute prior to a training jump in July 1973. Robinson and his fellow troopers are wearing the OG 107 utility uniform with black leather combat boots. Robinson had previously served in Vietnam, as evidenced by the divisional insignia worn on the right sleeve of his utility jacket. Interestingly, the patch is the black and olive drab 'subdued' variant. (NA)

Left: Troopers load onto a UH-60A helicopter at the start of an air assault exercise. The UH-60 is the successor of the UH-1 Huey. The troopers are all wearing the cotton and nylon Battle Dress Uniform (BDU), Temperate Zone, in woodland pattern camouflage. The man at the center is wearing the large nylon field pack, which can carry as much as 70 lbs. of equipment. (USA)

Opposite page, top: Two troopers practice rapelling at Fort Campbell. Both are wearing the BDU uniform with black leather jump boots and Type II Ml Paratrooper helmets. Note the full color airborne insignia on the left shoulder. The Airborne tab is now largely an honorary title as the division is now airmobile, not airborne. (USA)

Opposite page, bottom: Replacements to the division begin their instruction on how to properly rapel from a hovering helicopter at a simple wooden wall. Most of these recruits and their instructors are wearing the BDU uniform although one man is wearing olive green utilities. (USA)

Above: Although now an airmobile division, many members of the 101st are still jump qualified. Here, a trooper has just exited the door of an aircraft. The yellow static line of his T-10 parachute can be seen coming from the back of his parachute and attached to the interior of the aircraft. (USA)

Left: After landing a trooper must recover his parachute for repacking. The trooper is careful not to tangle his shroud lines or damage the canopy as he recovers the parachute.

Right: Troopers carefully check one another's equipment prior to a jump during Operation *Bright Star*. Both men are wearing their parachute harnesses over the daytime desert camouflage BDU uniform. The helmet on the man at right would indicate that he will probably be making a high altitude, low opening (HALO) jump. (USAF)

Below: Members of the division practice parachute landing falls (PLFs) at a class conducted during *Operation Desert Shield.* All of the men are wearing the daytime desert utility uniform with olive and black subdued insignia and personal armored system for ground troops (PASGT) Kevlar 'fritz' helmet. (USA)

Opposite page, top: A convoy of 101st high mobility, multipurpose-wheeled vehicles (HMMWV) Humvees' move across the Saudi Arabian desert. The Humvee is the replacement vehicle for the M151. As was common with their predecessors, these troopers have festooned their vehicles with all manner of personal equipment. (USA)

Opposite page, bottom: A driver of a 5 ton truck inspects his vehicle's .50 caliber machine gun. Although dating from World War II, the .50 caliber continues to be used on many of the Army's vehicles. (USA)

Right: Troopers set up their M224 60mm Lightweight Mortar. The M224 is issued to airborne divisions in lieu of the heavier 81mm mortar. The mortar can reach targets at ranges of up to 3,500 yards. These men are wearing BDU uniform and desert 'boonie' hats to shield their faces from the sun. (USA)

Below: A trooper cleans his Vulcan air defense gun with a brush. The Vulcan is a fully automatic 20mm cannon that can be mounted on either vehicles, as here, or on helicopters such as the Cobra gunship. Although devastating when working, the sensitive mechanisms on the Vulcan had to be frequently cleaned while in the desert. (USA)

Above: Comedian Steve Martin jokes with men of the division during a visit to Saudi Arabia. All of the men surrounding Martin are wearing the daytime desert BDUs with boonie hats. The man third from the right has chosen to wrap the cotton desert scarf around his neck. Although the troopers continue to wear standard olive drab and black subdued insignia, Martin has been able to obtain a tan and brown nametape that more closely matches the color scheme on his BDU jacket. (USA)

Below: A heavily laden Humvee towing a Vulcan air defense gun halts momentarily during the Allied advance across the desert during *Operation Desert Storm*. Visible on the back of the truck is a blaze orange airborne recognition panel. Despite such precautions, friendly fire was a recurring problem for Allied soldiers during the Persian Gulf War. (USA)

Above: The crew of an Apache helicopter work on their aircraft's weapon. The crewman at left wears BDU uniform with olive drab t-shirt, while his partner wears the fire retardant army aviation coveralls. Apache helicopters devastated Iraqi vehicle columns during *Operation Desert Storm*. (USA)

Below: The crew of an M102 105mm howitzer prepare to fire on Iraqi positions. This lightweight artillery piece had been in service with airborne and airmobile units since the Vietnam War. (USA)

A PFC with an AN/PRC 25 radio calls in for further instructions. His rank insignia is pinned to the front of his helmet. In his left hand he is holding the M16A2 rifle. Just visible at his left side is the carrier for his M17A2 gas mask. Fear of possible Iraqi use of chemical weapons required that all GIs serving in Saudi Arabia have their masks with them at all times. (USA)